Start TO Finish
Second Series

FROM Egg TO Ladybug

LISA OWINGS

LERNER PUBLICATIONS Minneapolis

Lerner Publications Company
A division of Lerner Publishing Group, Inc.
241 First Avenue North
Minneapolis, MN 55401 USA

For reading levels and more information, look up this title at www.lernerbooks.com.

Library of Congress Cataloging-in-Publication Data

Names: Owings, Lisa, author.
Title: From egg to ladybug / Lisa Owings.
Other titles: Start to finish (Minneapolis, Minn.). Second series.
Description: Minneapolis : Lerner Publications, [2016] | Series: Start to finish. Second series | Audience: Ages 5–9. | Audience: K to grade 3. | Includes bibliographical references and index.
Identifiers: LCCN 2015036522| ISBN 9781512409109 (lb : alk. paper) | ISBN 9781512412987 (pb : alk. paper) | ISBN 9781512410822 (eb pdf)
Subjects: LCSH: Ladybugs—Life cycles—Juvenile literature. | Life cycles (Biology)—Juvenile literature.
Classification: LCC QL596.C65 O95 2016 | DDC 595.76/9—dc23

LC record available at http://lccn.loc.gov/2015036522

Manufactured in the United States of America
1 – CG – 7/15/16

TABLE OF Contents

First, a ladybug finds a place for her eggs. 4

She lays her eggs in a cluster. 6

Soon the eggs hatch into larvae. 8

Each larva eats the food around it. 10

Then the larva grows and sheds its skin. 12

Next, the larva becomes a pupa. 14

The pupa's body changes shape. 16

Finally, the adult ladybug emerges. 18

The new ladybug helps keep away pests! 20

Glossary 22

Further Information 23

Index 24

I like ladybugs!

How do they grow?

First, a ladybug finds a place for her eggs.

A ladybug is ready to lay her eggs. She carefully chooses a place near a **colony** of **aphids** or other small insects. Later, these insects will be food for her young.

She lays her eggs in a cluster.

The ladybug lays a cluster of eggs. The eggs are long and golden. Most will hatch in a few days. Some of the eggs are **unfertilized** and will not hatch. Any unhatched eggs will be food for the hatchlings.

Soon the eggs hatch into larvae.

After three to five days, larvae hatch from their eggs. A ladybug larva looks a bit like a tiny alligator. It is dark and spiny with bright patches. It immediately starts looking for food.

Each larva eats the food around it.

The larva races to eat the unhatched eggs before its siblings do. Then it goes hunting for aphids and other **pests**. It can eat dozens of aphids per day.

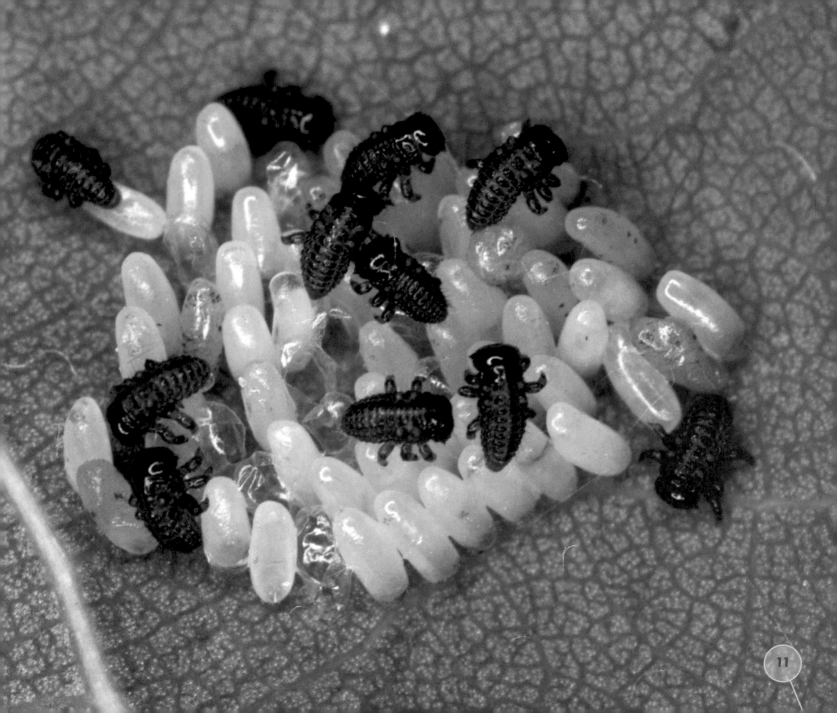

Then the larva grows and sheds its skin.

The larva grows and grows. It sheds its tough
skin so its body can grow even bigger. The larva
molts several times over the following weeks.

Next, the larva becomes a pupa.

The larva's last molt reveals a pupa. The pupa attaches its tail to a leaf. The rest of its shellfish-like body twists and shakes as it **transforms**.

The pupa's body changes shape.

Within the pupa's skin, the adult ladybug takes shape. Its long, spiny body becomes round and smooth. Wings form under a shiny shell. The skin of the pupa turns dark orange with black spots.

Finally, the adult ladybug emerges.

In a week or two, the adult ladybug is fully formed. It sheds its skin one last time. But it doesn't look like a ladybug quite yet. Its body is soft and pale. Soon the shell hardens and takes on its familiar bright, spotted appearance.

The new ladybug helps keep away pests!

The adult ladybug flies away to find food. Its appetite for pests helps farmers and gardeners. Soon it will **mate** and the life cycle will begin again.

Glossary

aphids: tiny insects that harm plants

colony: a group of animals or insects that live together

emerges: comes out from a hidden place

larvae: insects whose stage of growth is between egg and pupa. *Larvae* is plural for *larva*.

mate: join together to produce young

molts: loses an old covering of skin, fur, or feathers to make way for a new covering

pests: insects or animals that harm crops and other animals

pupa: the stage of an insect's growth between larva and adult

transforms: completely changes

unfertilized: unable to grow and develop

Further Information

Glaser, Linda. *Not a Buzz to Be Found: Insects in Winter.* Minneapolis: Millbrook Press, 2012. Ever wonder what ladybugs and other insects do in winter? Read this book to find out!

Jenkins, Steve. *The Beetle Book.* Boston: Houghton Mifflin Books for Children, 2012. Did you know ladybugs are actually beetles? This book tells all about them with fun illustrations.

Mattern, Joanne. *It's a Good Thing There Are Ladybugs.* New York: Children's Press, 2015. Grab this book to find out how ladybugs are good for Earth.

National Geographic Kids: Ladybug
http://kids.nationalgeographic.com/animals/ladybug
Check out this site for fun facts and photos about ladybugs.

San Diego Zoo Kids: Ladybug
http://kids.sandiegozoo.org/animals/insects/ladybug
Learn about ladybugs, and enjoy fun games and activities on this site.

Index

aphids, 4, 10

eggs, 4–10

food, 4–10, 20

larvae, 8

pests, 10, 20
pupa, 14–16

skin, 12, 16–18
spots, 16–18

Photo Acknowledgments
The images in this book are used with the permission of:
© Graphic Science/Alamy, pp. 1, 5; © irin-k/Shutterstock.
com, p. 3; © imageBROKER /Alamy, p. 7; © PHOTO FUN/
Shutterstock.com, pp. 9, 17; © Patti Murray/Animals
Animals, p. 11; © Gilles San Martin/Wikimedia Commons,
p. 13; © antos777/Shutterstock.com, p. 15; © E.R.
Degginger/Getty Images, p. 19; © Marcin Niemiec/
Shutterstock.com, p. 21.

Front cover: © Yellowj/Shutterstock.com.

Main body text set in Arta Std Book 20/26.
Typeface provided by International Typeface Corp.

LERNER
e
SOURCE

Expand learning beyond the printed book. Download free, complementary educational resources for this book from our website, www.lerneresource.com.